Published in the USA by
BearManor Media
1317 Edgewater Dr. #110
Orlando, FL 32804
www.BearManorMedia.com

Softcover Edition
ISBN: 978-1-62933-655-8

Printed in the United States of America

My Funny Valentine:
A Tribute to My Mother,
Ann Sothern

by Tisha Sterling

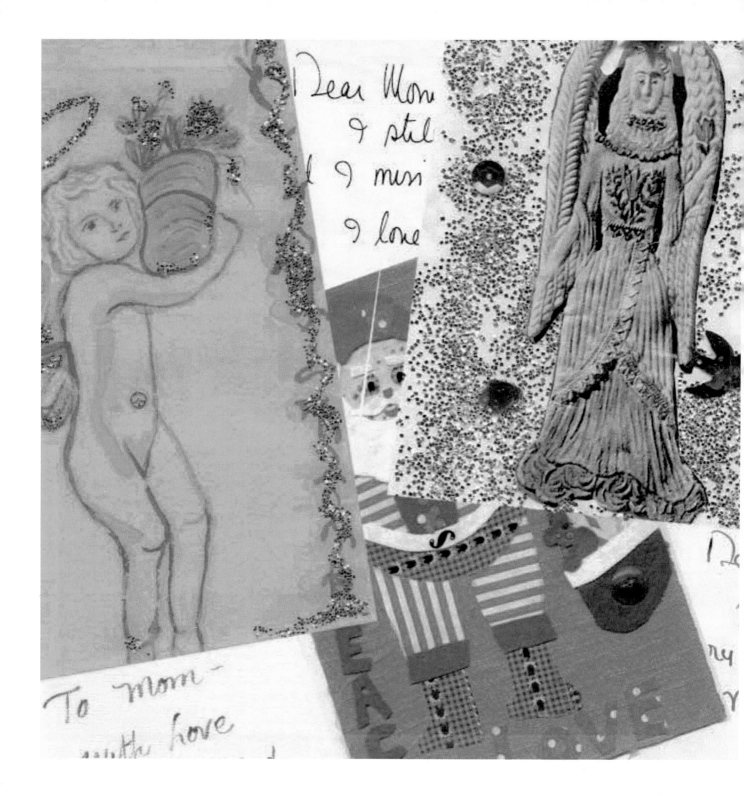

Dear Mom
I stil...
...I I miss
I love

To mom -
with love

S hortly after December 10, 1944, my mother, Ann Sothern, wrote a rather lengthy piece for a movie magazine: "*A Valentine to My Beautiful Daughter Tisha.*" It was a letter to me, expressing her love, hopes, and dreams for me. Included were the first pictures of us together, me in her arms, and photos of the whole family, including my father, actor Robert Sterling. I still have the article. Some years later, after my mother's death in 2001, as I was sorting through the huge trunks full of photographs, letters, journals, and memorabilia documenting her life and the times she lived in, it was as if a whole world of her past through nine decades was revealing itself again. Suddenly I was inspired to respond to her valentine, and honor my mother at the end of her life, as she had honored me at my beginning.

This book, then, is that valentine, dedicated to Miss Ann Sothern—born Harriet Lake—a famous American lady, and my mother. To the world, she lived a huge Hollywood-style life, having a presence and quality that was completely unique. Music was at the core, and she had a huge talent. She could dance, sing, act, and be funny. She achieved fame first on stage, then the movies, and finally on television—a feat accomplished by very few actors and even fewer actresses—culminating in an Academy Award nomination for *Whales of August* in 1987, when she was seventy-eight years old.

Mother became a star at a time when stars were fewer and better loved than they are now. She was independent, a self-made woman in Hollywood who was never taken care of by a man. She made all of her own money, produced her own television series long before Mary Tyler Moore, and loved to live high on the fruits of her labor. And labor she did. I can only guess at the trials she must have endured during the thirties and forties, when Hollywood was more misogynistic than it is today. But my mother always had the ability to talk to men in a way that made them feel at ease with themselves, while still getting her way almost every time. This was a skill perhaps cultivated in the process of building a career in the backslapping, boys club of pre-adolescent Hollywood. She was, in a word, a feminist—before there were feminists.

A part of the visual valentine I offer now is in appreciation of my mother's career: for the courage, stamina, and sacrifice this kind of achievement demands, especially for a woman. Though successful, she was extremely underappreciated in Hollywood—especially later in her life—for her real and very different personality, as well as for the astonishing and varied body of work she left behind (64 movies, 175 TV episodes). It is my valentine gift to honor her unique talent and legacy.

The other part of this valentine is for who my mother was as a person, and the life we shared together. We sent each other countless cards and valentines over the years—some loving, some bitter with jealousy and pride, some dripping with remorse. But all, in the end, written out of love, or at least a desire to love each other in the way that would make the other feel loved. Even during my wildest days as a privileged hippie and at the height of addiction in my thirties, I sent Mother "I still love you even though everything's all screwed up" cards. To everyone's astonishment, I moved away from Hollywood to be near my mother, following her to Sun Valley, Idaho. In all honesty, and although I was not aware of it at the time, I was afraid to let go of her. When she became debilitated after a terrible accident onstage, I cared for her, with the help of many others, until she died.

This is a mother-and-daughter's American Hollywood tale, spanning the ninety-two years of Ann Sothern's life. It also tells the story of a rapidly changing America. I've tried to weave the fabric of these decades through words and images in this book. I've also tried to paint the picture of my mother and myself as real women, allowing for the tragic truths implicit in everyone's life, and the humor and lessons that emerged. My mother was definitely on a journey. Spiritually, she started at one place and ended in another. It is my intention to trace that sometimes complicated but ultimately rewarding path. For part of loving someone is accepting their frailties. At the end of my mother's life, there was a deeper love between us which clearly emerged and transformed both of us. This valentine honors that transformation.

Thank you for taking this journey with me.

Tisha

The Forties

Meeting Robert Sterling

WWII

The Ideal Marriage

Homecoming

A New Daughter

Final Divorce

The Independent Actress

Ann

1942

Filming one of the Maisie series, *Ringside Maisie*, my mother met a member of the cast, the handsome up-and-coming actor Robert Sterling. They fell madly in love.

1942

During the Forties, Mother had a small coterie of best friends. Together they shared a sunny camaraderie. They shared in the joy of their husbands being home from the war, their children, their careers and long sunny days in Los Angeles when the air was clean and it was a beautiful safe haven. It was a special time, much more like a community. When she spoke of these times, I never got the sense that they were terribly competitive among each other. They gossiped like crazy, since I'm sure there was a lot to talk about. They enjoyed each other's company and zany humor. They loved picnics, and went roller skating all over Beverly Hills. They gave their children birthday and Christmas parties that are hard to define in the real world. Tables strewn with magical fabrics, and a beautiful cake. Clowns to entertain us, making funny animal shapes with balloons, and real ponies to ride. Santa Claus would always appear at Christmastime and stories were read, and movies like *Bambi* and *Snow White* were shown. They had their cocktails in Steuben crystal glasses and wore their beautiful clothes and hats . . . . They had natural beauty about them, a sort of shiny quality like a tinted photograph. To me, no one has ever looked the same, or had that very special aura about them.

1942

My parents, Ann Sothern (born Harriet Lake), and Robert Sterling (born William J. Hart), married on May 23, 1943, nine short days after Mother's divorce from Roger Pryor was official. My mother was already a star, and was filming *Cry Havoc,* one of the movies she shot in between the hugely successful *Maisie* films. Pop was also under contract with MGM and moving up the ladder. They were such a glamorous Hollywood couple. Mother took two days' leave from the set to get married. When she returned, the cast gave her a "ration wedding shower." The U.S. was in the middle of a war it still didn't know it would win, and both my mother and father were doing what they could for the war effort. Mom had joined the USO, visiting wounded servicemen and entertaining the troops. During that time, she became a favorite WWII pin-up girl, even having a plane named "Maisie" in her honor. And Dad was teaching flying in a flight school in Pecos, Texas. Like so many marriages during the war, my parents' was impulsive and dangerous. They knew the war would separate them as soon as they were married. But the unsure world seemed to take the fear of commitment away. Though rushed, Mother of course wanted the wedding ceremony to have style. She made sure the orchid she wore as a corsage matched her three-quarter-length fuchsia gloves.

WESTERN UNION

CLASS OF SERVICE

This is a full-rate Telegram or Cablegram unless its deferred character is indicated by a suitable symbol above or preceding the address.

A. N. WILLIAMS
PRESIDENT

NEWCOMB CARLTON
CHAIRMAN OF THE BOARD

J. C. WILLEVER
FIRST VICE-PRESIDENT

1201

(44)

SYMBOLS

DL = Day Letter

NL = Night Letter

LC = Deferred Cable

NLT = Cable Night Letter

Ship Radiogram

The filing time shown in the date line on telegrams and day letters is STANDARD TIME at point of origin. Time of receipt is STANDARD TIME at point of destination

SW 34 17=WUX PECOS TEX 23 904A

MRS ROBERT STERLING=   1943 JUL 23 AM 8 47

=723 NORTH CRESCENT DR BEVERLYHILLS CALIF=

DARLING: BOND,OF MAY 23RD WONDERFUL AND BEAUTIFUL ONLY WISH

I COULD BE THERE TODAY AND ALWAYS=

=MR S.

.23 S.

THE COMPANY WILL APPRECIATE SUGGESTIONS FROM ITS PATRONS CONCERNING ITS SERVICE

1943

1943

After my mother's death, I found a steel box that had been locked for many, many years. When I pried it open, I found love letters to my father. While reading them, the depth of her feeling for him suddenly came alive again. I was shocked that Mother had kept the letters, for it meant she really cared about Pop. She had a saying:"I just close the door." And after she and pop were no more, that's exactly what she did, but she did not lock her heart.

Monday--

Pookie Darling!

Here is the key to our grip, which is on its way to you by Railway Express. Don't worry about the grip getting dirty sweetheart, cause I've got another slip cover for it—for when we need it on our "elegant" travels. It's locked, darling- so be careful of its key, won't you? Also I'm doing something else for you, baby. Bob Taylor told me all about it—and I thought it was such a good idea, I'm doing it for you.

He has sent all his clothes (not shirts, ties, etc.) but street clothes to the Peerless Laundry, where they have a special storage service for Service Men. They are completely demothed— they hang upright, they're insured—and taken care of perfectly. I've worried about your things being so packed into that trunk downstairs—and moths get into them so easily—and being in there so long—so I'm taking it upon myself to do this, baby. So when you come back—we'll <u>know</u> they're all right. There are only six suits—and I'm valuing them at $150.00 apiece. Is that right, darling? And the cost is very cheap—2% of the value per month, I think. Anyway, it's not expensive. And it's good assurance, darling. I guess that's all I have to tell you right now, baby.

It was wonderful to talk to you yesterday sweetheart—and I love you to pieces! Watty and Jerry were over last night, and we all talked about you so much! Have to go now honey—<u>please</u> be so careful—and I'm so proud of you, baby!

I <u>love</u> being Mrs. Robert Sterling more than anything in the world!

All my love—dearest.

M ["M" stood for Moushka, Pop's nickname for her.]

BEATITUDES FOR HUSBANDS

1. Blessed is the husband who is thoughtful of many little things, for his wife shall never complain.

2. Blessed is the husband who is not miserly, for his wife shall be as a sweet-scented plant in his home.

3. Blessed is the husband who is not selfish, for his wife and children will love him without measure.

4. Blessed is the husband who is not a chronic gambler, for his wife shall have peace of mind.

5. Blessed is the husband who maketh not his wife a " sports widow", for he will be cherished even unto his old age.

6. Blessed is the husband who is not a "sot", for he will be esteemed even on this earth.

7. Blessed is the husband who gives good example, for his wife and children shall not be scandalized in him.

8. Blessed is the husband who loves his wife and will have traffic with no other, for he is a man after God's own heart.

This little poem, found amidst mom's cherished love letters, told the story of the expectations of a husband during the forties and the fifties. The expectations of husband and wife were not easily met in those days. Mom didn't exactly fit the typical forties' wife. She was independent, had a huge career, and made her own money. And Dad wasn't the perfect forties' husband either, spending most of his time at the Bel-Air Country Club.

"Tisha honey," she said. "One day I just ran off to the gynecologist's office for that little paper book that told you how to tell when you were ovulating. I followed it right down to the T! You had to take your temperature several times a day, which was a bore, but I was just so intent on this happening for me, so excited. I was mad for your father and I wanted a child so badly. It was during the war, and your father was stationed way the hell up in Sacramento. I really had to get things going . . . it was important that the timing be just right! I got the beautiful old Lincoln out and left practically in the middle of the night! Thank God, I got there at just the right time in the afternoon. And everything just turned out perfectly . . ." She said this as if she were a teenager. It made me laugh.

Patricia Ann Sterling,
born December 10,
1944.
I was two weeks late. Mom
said she had to drink a lot
of castor oil to "blast me
out."

1946

There was a huge old sycamore tree in front of our house in the Hollywood Hills, it's three trunks branching out in different directions, one trunk for each of us: Mom, Pop, and Me. My dad had just returned from the war. Mom was ecstatic, and relieved, to have him home. There was hope everywhere, even filtering through the leaves of that tree. The day this photograph was taken, we were all connected—I was standing on my father's foot, and was leaning against my mother for support. She was gently balancing me with her hand on my arm. Her other arm was around my father's waist. And his hand was cupped on her behind. I did not know that six months later, my father would be gone.

1948

N either my mother nor father ever discussed the reasons for the their divorce with me. But I do know that one day, Helen Connolly, Mom's decorator, came to the house and told her that her gardener had heard a rumor that Dad had a crush on a long-legged dancer, and was following her around. On January 2, 1948, they were separated, and then divorced in 1949. When I ask my father about that period, he will only say, "Tisha, you're asking me about a very, very difficult time." And Mom would only say, "He was impossible." Mom had great friends to get her through the transition, and Caesar Romero, known to his friends as "Butch," was one of the mainstays in my mother's life. He and my mother's best friend, Mal Milland, Ray Milland's wife, consoled her and took care of her through the divorce.

This was Mother in the film *April Showers*. She sang the title song with wistful sweetness. It is a simple song about hope and having no regrets.

When I was small, I was in awe of her beauty, of all the things she used to wear: the garter belts and silk underwear, the way her petticoat rustled, the funny and outrageous hats that framed her face, the way her satin shoes sounded on the set, her red lipstick, and her scent—like non-filtered Luckies and Guerlain, Mitsouko, L'Heure Bleu, Shalimar… I will always associate those perfumes with her.

Mother took me to the studio as much as she could. I loved dressing up, and was on my best behavior. Maybe I could meet the Lion or the Tin Man, or see the Prince! My mother loved acting. She bloomed when doing her work. It was who she was. She had that rare star quality that compelled people to watch only her.

The post-war experiment of settling down as Mrs. Robert Sterling having been a disappointment, Mom accepted the role of a ferociously independent woman. She was never again to exude the kind of soft playfulness she had enjoyed during her early married years. She was now a worker and a breadwinner. As she'd to say to me, she wasn't *Mrs. Wiggs of the Cabbage Patch*, never the long-suffering hausfrau.

Though April showers may come your way,
They bring the flowers that bloom in May.
So if it's raining, have no regrets.
Because it isn't raining rain, you know...
It's raining violets.

And where you see clouds up on the hill,
You soon will see crowds of daffodils.
So keep on looking for a bluebird,
And listening for his song,
Whenever April showers come along.

Buddy DeSylva and Lewis Silvers

There has always been a huge painting in our houses, a portrait by Paul Clemens of my mother and myself. When I went to the Clemens studio in Hollywood, I was required to climb up onto a ledge, and to sit perfectly still. When I allow myself to walk deeply into this Renoir-like painting, I can still feel how my new pink petticoat itched, and how I wanted to take it off. I wanted to jump down and play away from her. Yet there I sat like the good girl, loving the nearness of her whole being. And my mother sat tall and proud in her blue satin dress, exuding the great beauty she was. I sat patiently next to her on those hot Hollywood days, squeezing our Siamese cat until she hissed at me.

1948.

When I was just five, I was told my mother was going away for awhile to a hospital where she would stay until she was better. I was scared. I wondered what she was doing there. My nanny lied and told me there was going to be a new baby in the house.

At the end of the film called *Nancy Goes to Rio*, my mother was invited to go to England for that year's Command Performance, an annual gathering of movie stars who would sing and dance in a fabulous musical review for the Royal family. It was considered a great honor. Among the stars performing that year were Rosiland Russell, Myrna Loy, Michael Wilding, and Cary Grant. This year's theme was "A Christmas Special." Mother had opted out of this event for three years, but this time, at the last minute, the studio and her agent insisted that she go. So, with only one week to prepare, she rushed to the doctor to get the series of shots one got for going overseas. This included a smallpox vaccination.

In England, mother was a smash. She met the Queen  and Prince Philip, and like everyone else, was entranced by the Royals. But back in her room, she began to feel peculiarly claustrophobic. When the London fog crept under the doors at the Savoy Hotel, she felt edgy and caged in. She attributed these sensations to overall fatigue. But when she left England for France, she found the same creepy claustrophobia overcoming her.

After returning to Los Angles, she escaped to Sun Valley, Idaho, needing a good rest. As she was boarding the old Union Pacific train that left downtown Los Angeles, she found that she could not bear to be inside the train itself. She backed down the station stairs and went home. The next day, she managed to get on an airplane and fly into Sun Valley, the famous ski resort owned by Averell Harriman, the former governor of New York and ambassador to France. It was my mother's favorite place in the world, because she could let her hair down.

After a few days in Idaho, she felt better. It was time to ski. After an hour on the slopes, she collapsed. She had to be taken down the hill on a toboggan. After a careful examination, she was told that she had the worst case of hepatitis her doctors had ever seen. The virus had been hidden in Mother's smallpox vaccination. It was the vaccine which nearly wiped out a battalion at Guantanamo Bay.

1952

ANN SOTHERN

STARRING IN

"Private Secretary"

A HALF HOUR TV FILM PRESENTATION

The Fifties

When mother re-created herself on television as Susie McNamara, the liberated queen of all secretaries in *Private Secretary*, she was also creating a new offscreen persona: producer. Television production was a new art, rather slow and clunky, and mother brought a lot of new ideas to the forefront. She wanted a reasonable nine-to-six shooting schedule, instead of the usual ten-or-twelve-hour norm for a series at that time. To save time, Mother had the idea of flying the scenery like they did in the theater. She also asked the studio to create a smooth floor made of cement, almost glasslike, so that cameras could be moved easily and quickly around the set. One of the biggest innovations, though, was air conditioning. The sets of that time were excruciatingly hot, but not on *Private Secretary*. Actors and crew from sweltering sets all over the studio would come to the *PS* set to cool off. It had the feeling of a party. Everyone had more energy and room to breathe, so they were happier and more productive.

It wasn't easy being the second woman (Lucy was the first) to produce her own TV show. My mother irritated major studio executives with her new and independent ideas. She was awarded the title "Little Miss MGM" for her innovations, and to a degree, her reputation as demanding put her in the realm of lonely pioneers. Some people didn't want to work with her anymore. But because of the time Mom saved on the set, we got a chance to have dinner together most nights and talk about our days. Our favorite dessert was floating islands. Her show was a smashing success. Hooray Mom!

1952

Each morning at 7 a.m., a driver would fetch my mother and take her to the Desilu Studio on Santa Monica and Gower for a day's work of *Private Secretary*. Many times I would accompany her, and spend the day at the studio watching all the goings-on. She was very strong inside, and completely engaged in the work, yet she was gracious and kind to everyone on the set. My mother's strength was the wind that blew the project along, and her humor the glue that held it together. She seemed to be flying at this time, free and strong, soaring, steadily riding the winds of success. I was tied to the end of my mother's kite.

What a pair of rare birds these two women were! And great pals! Mother told me many times how much she loved Lucille. They made each other laugh. Lucy, so vibrant and vivacious on the screen, found a safe place in her friendship with my mother. Mother accepted Lucy's quiet and private self. Their friendship flourished from the thirties when they appeared together as very young women in *Kid Millions,* *Broadway Thru a Keyhole,* and *As Thousands Cheer.* Their most endearing times together professionally were in the fifties on their TV shows *I Love Lucy* ("Lucy Takes a Cruise to Havana"), *Private Secretary, The Ann Sothern Show, and The Lucy Show.* These two completely individual women knew how to do everything: song, dance, drama, comedy—you name it. When they worked together, it was a fun and loving collaboration.

M other said she was a great straight man
for Lucy, and that's why they worked so
well as a team. They weren't afraid to try anything.
Both of them had an amazing mastery of timing.
Each entered a frame with superb nonchalance.
No one ever took a film or television show away
from them. Yet they were very giving and helpful
to other cast members. A lot of actors got their
first breaks on their shows. They were generous
that way, and not in any way competitive with each
other.

Mother said the only time she ever butted
heads with her friend was during an episode of
The Lucy Show when Lucille was giving a certain
director a pretty harsh dressing-down for his inter-
pretation of a scene. My mother became uncom-
fortable and embarrassed for the director and
walked off the set to go to her dressing room until
things quieted down. After a while, Lucy noticed
my mother's absence and she was ready to go back
to work . . . "Will you puh-leeze go and ask the
great Ms. Sothern if she would reappear on the
set?" My mother came back, but I think the fact
that she had left the set embarrassed Lucille. But,
egos intact and their love and respect for one
another foremost in their hearts, work resumed.

I bet they're having fun in heaven teaching Gabriel how to do a prat fall.

In 1987, my mother received her first Academy Award nomination for her 70th film, *The Whales of August.* It had been ten years since my mother had made a motion picture, and she had been lonely before the start of this film, fighting pain in her body and living isolated in Idaho. The quality of lonliness illuminates her performance.

The papers called the cast a gathering of "Royalty," and indeed it was, with the likes of Lillian Gish, Bette Davis, Vincent Price, Harry Carey Jr., and its distinguished director, Lindsey Anderson.

The story is about aging sisters, played by Miss Gish and Miss Davis—one caring for the other—and of their best friend and neighbor, Tisha, played by my mother. It was poignantly, delicately told. The sparsity of action and talk are counterbalanced with the power to touch an audience and the dignity of the performances.

"God, all of us," my mother said of the cast, "we have all been at it for a LONG time." What true words.

I think my mother was proud that I was included in this, her last film, to be playing her as a young woman. It was also a strange coincidence that her character's name in the film was Tisha. Among other things, it was that coincidence which motivated her to take the role. But I know she loved the part and the screenplay and was longing to work again. My mother was always the actress. She did it out of the need to be creative.

At the time, I was going through a particularly bad patch, and she helped me a great deal by urging the producers to consider me for the role. I was honored to get the part.

S hewas particularly fond of Lilian Gish. Really, she was in awe of her. One moment on the set, my mother was overheard whispering, "It's an honor to act with you, darling." And on a day when some of the last shots were being filmed, my mother made a little speech: "I've done a lot of movies, but never with a more solicitous and dedicated crew then you guys. I've had a wonderful time, and I'll never forget you."

"And we'll never forget you!" responded Lillian.

As she was leaving the set after the last shot, she said, "How do we know that this is not going to be the last hurrah for all of us."

O n the evening of the Academy awards, all of us were excited and expectant .We were in the second row at the Dorothy Chandler Pavilion. My mother looked radiant. Her dear friend Mike Kaplan, producer of *The Whales of August*, was sitting to her right, I was to her left, and my daughter Heidi was next to me. They announced the Best

Supporting Actress . . . it was not she. She was crushed. She simply asked me if I would hand over her sunglasses from her purse. She put them on, looked straight ahead and never said a word. I was brokenhearted for her. We never discussed it. It was too hard. I just wish a million times over she would have won. She deserved it.

It was hard for me to see my mother change and grow old. Quite suddenly it seemed, our roles reversed—I was expected to be the adult and she became in many ways like a child. My mother had always been so strong and seemingly in charge of her environment. She had always been so active. Always making her own decisions. Yet all these qualities changed dramatically as she grew older and increasingly dependent.

The last ten years of her life, she suffered greatly from physical pain. Although she still loved to paint, her vision had deteriorated. Her style of artwork, like her personality, had been multifaceted. She had been a painter of portraits and character studies, simple paintings of old-fashioned women standing by the sea, as well as big colorful pastels of different American Indian tribes. Her hands had always busy with needlepoint. Now they were increasingly still.

She lost her hearing for music and piano. Her musical repertoire, which had filled the house so sweetly, was quieted. Conversations no longer titillated her, so our parlor was no longer filled with the usual lively group. Daily events and holidays no longer thrilled her, and it was evident to me that the external world had lost much of its meaning.

The practicalities of caring for my mother filled me with anxiety. Just finding the caregivers who could deal with her needs was extremely challenging. Many of them were wonderful and patient people, but some were not. This utterly frustrated and angered me, but ultimately it taught me great patience. It helped me to gain a much larger, more humorous and more tolerant understanding of human nature. In the end, a wonderful woman named Attie came into our lives to help shepherd my mom through some of her most difficult times. I believe she was sent to us by God, as I was pretty much at the end of my rope when she came. There were many others who helped me through this time with their wisdom and support. An artist friend of mine, whose mother lived with her to the ripe old age of a hundred, told me that rather than resent the additional responsibility of caring for our parents, we must rejoice in their lives, as they are truly living through her own karma here on earth. It is my humble opinion that my mother was learning about pride and the letting go of it.

When my mother died that gray March day, I felt like a transparent little aspen leaf one often sees stuck by the sides of old buildings, crushed and forgotten, ready to be blown to the winds. She had been the central figure of my life and now she was gone. Our lives had been a tapestry of bittersweet closeness and estrangement.

The day after she died, my son-in-law, Greg, and my daughter Heidi and I were outside looking up into the tallest tree in my mother's huge yard. On the uppermost branch of this enormous and ancient tree sat a huge horned owl! I looked toward my daughter and exclaimed, "That's Mom! Hello Mom," and the great owl hooted at us once or twice. Then it spread its wings and flew closely over our heads. It was as if to say, "I love you, my girls, but I am off now. I am free and flying away." They say owls represent the feminine, death, protection, and the letting go of secrets. I have many owls in my house.

You taught me so much.

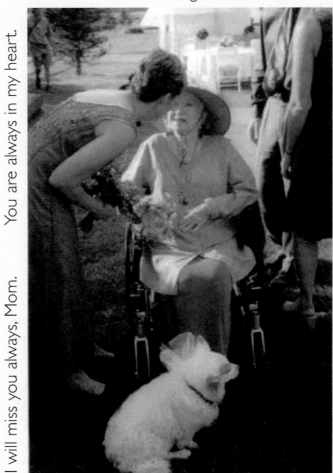

You are always in my heart.

I will miss you always, Mom.

Made in the USA
Middletown, DE
25 November 2021

53417807R00033